THE DUCKBOY WAY

or

Quack in the Saddle Again

by

Paul Stanton

DUCKBOY CARDS

For Laurie,

the original Duckgirl

≈

Published by Duckboy Cards, Milltown, Montana,
in cooperation with SkyHouse Publishers,
an imprint of Falcon Press®, Helena, Montana.

Library of Congress Catalog Card Number 97-65254

ISBN 1-883364-09-4

Distributed by Duckboy Cards
P.O. Box 86, Milltown, Montana 59851,
phone 1-800-761-5741,

and Falcon Press®, P.O. Box 1718, Helena, Montana 59624,
phone 1-800-582-2665.

First Edition

Manufactured in Canada.

Acknowledgments

I'm much obliged to those people who suggested photo ideas over the years, whether they were ever used or not. To the many "good sports" who have allowed me to photograph them in ridiculous and sometimes uncomfortable situations, I give my sincere thanks.

Thanks to Wes Selby for converting "The Duckboy Song" to sheet music for this book, and to Mike Gouse for his whimsical drawings, including the Duckboy logo.

For their expertise and patience in converting my images to cards, calendars, and promotional materials, I'm grateful to the folks at Color World Printers in Bozeman, Montana; and Gateway Printing in Missoula, Montana. Special thanks go to our faithful distributors, reps, and retailers, who make our products available to the public.

Also, a tip of the hat to our new friends at Falcon Press Publishing, who made this book happen.

Introduction

One snowy December day in Hamilton, Montana when I was nine or ten, I watched Dad outside our window picking roses. They were plastic. He'd wired them onto the frozen rosebushes days before, and was leisurely picking them for the benefit of passing traffic. He said one guy "nearly ran off the road gawking." Dad took his joking seriously.

My father and my two older brothers introduced me to snipe hunting, sidehill-gougers (a myth-illogical beast), uses for rubber dog doo, and "pull my finger." It was only fitting that I should carry on, and expand upon, a family tradition.

In high school, I loved the outdoors, photography, and satire. My senior year I led the unsuccessful effort for a drive-in graduation ceremony. I rode a Cushman scooter named "The Roaring Red Dog," complete with a tail, teeth, eyes, and floppy ears that rose up like wings when the machine reached its 40 mph top speed. With classmates I organized Hamilton's first "Junior Mister Pageant," featuring guys in evening wear (nightshirts and nightcaps) and sportswear (snowshoes, badminton rackets, swim fins, and snorkels). In a break with pageant tradition, contestants were expected to attack and "beat up" the winner. As it happened, I won.

During those years I often visited Ernst Peterson, a photographer whose studio was across the street from our family's grocery store. Ernst was well-known for his black-and-white photographs and photo-murals (often hand-colored) of scenery and wildlife in Montana and the Northwest. "The Story of the West in Pictures" was his theme. Ernst put up with my many questions, and taught me much about nature photography and hand-coloring. He believed that any picture taken on film smaller than a 4"x5" sheet was a "snapshot." In later years he sold me his 4"x5" Beseler enlarger, which I still use.

In college I studied still and movie photography. I worked in those fields for a while, but couldn't find a way to do them full-time while remaining in Montana.

My scenic black-and-white and hand-colored prints drew some praise at art fairs, but few buyers. To my surprise, the goofy photo-postcards I'd originally made up for my friends kept selling out. Individually printing each card in the darkroom took too much time. In 1987, with my wife Laurie's urging and support, I hired a commercial printer to produce a few thousand cards and I put them in two stores. They sold out quickly, and suddenly I was in the postcard business.

The name "Duckboy" came from the "Duckboy Song," which is on page 10. I wrote it in 1984 after I saw a flooded corral full of ducks in Wise River, Montana. I thought about how the West would be different had Americans preferred duck to beef. We'd have song titles like "I'm an Old Duck Hand from the Rio Grande," "Lonesome Quacker Call,"

or "Duck Drovers in the Sky." The Duckboy Song became popular on Montana public radio, especially on the kids' program.

Laurie joined the card business full-time within two years. Her help and expertise has allowed us to expand into all the western states, plus Minnesota. We now sell calendars and refrigerator magnets, along with a growing card line.

People often ask me where the photo ideas come from, and where we get our models. Many ideas are suggested by people who buy our cards. Some suggestions are great. Other ideas are adaptations of old jokes, or are dreamed up by me. Some we just happen upon, like seeing a bearded man named "Tex" riding a longhorn steer ("Tex's Longhorn Cow Pony," page 97) or a chair sitting in a lake ("Waiting for Breakfast," page 80).

Our models are people we know or meet. Nearly all our friends and relatives have been drafted into a postcard photo. When traveling, we often hire models in cafes, bars, bakeries, or state employment agencies. Our employee Scott has recruited many of his friends.

Shooting can be memorable. For convenience, we staged "Uphill Bobsled Team" (page 33) near the freeway entrance in Missoula. By the time we finished, there were six or seven carloads of spectators parked nearby, waiting for the rocket sled to blast off up the hill. When the fireworks didn't occur, they drove off in disgust.

A game warden checked up on us while I was photographing "Catch and Release Fishing Out West" (page 49). Fishing season was closed, but giant fiberglass bass don't count. I'm sure he had a good story when he got back to the office.

For the "Downhill Golfing in Colorado" photo, Laurie's Uncle Jack teed off on the ski hill at Winter Park. Jack drew wisecracks from skiers on the chair lift, such as, "Use your wedge!" "Can we play through?" and "What's your handicap?"

After ten years in the card business, it's satisfying to assemble a selection of my photos and stories into this book. We hope you enjoy coming on this little photographic snipe hunt as much as we've enjoyed bringing you along.

DOWNHILL GOLFING IN COLORADO

WATCHING BEARS CHASE JOGGERS . . . A GROWING SPECTATOR SPORT

TROLLING FOR MOUNTAIN LIONS

Duckboy Song

Words and Music ©1984 Paul Stanton (BMI)

Arr. by Wesley T. Selby

I'm an old duck dro-ver from out in Mon-tan-a I round up them quackers and drive 'em a-long To a flooded cor-ral where we bull-dog and brand 'em And mos-ey on home just a-sing-in' this song:

REFRAIN

Singin' quack quack yippee aay_____ quack quack yippie oh! git a-long lit-tle

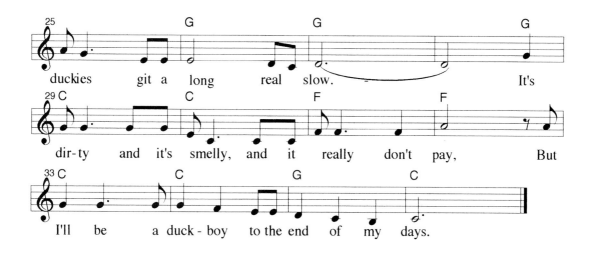

duckies git a long real slow. It's
dir-ty and it's smelly, and it really don't pay, But
I'll be a duck - boy to the end of my days.

2nd verse   On Saturday nights I ride into town
On my shortlegged pony, with my hat pulled 'way down.
But the girls don't like duckboys, an' I can't figger why—
No cowboy could be more romantic than I.

(refrain)

3rd verse   There's danger, adventure, and romance I know . . .
From a waddlin' stampede, to the duck rodeo.
But there's loneliness too, and it cuts to the bone;
When ya smell like duck feathers, you're always alone.

(refrain)

Memoirs of an Old Duckboy

As told by Spud Fisk, the "Toughest Old Coot in the Bitterroot"
Drawings by Mike Gouse

I was on the last big duck roundup and trail drive in Western Montana. It was 1923. Me, Soapy Swanson, and 25 other duckboys drove 16 thousand quackers from Lima north to the NP railhead at Twin Bridges. Folks along the way could see the dust for five miles and hear the quacking for ten. Being a duckboy was always dirty work, especially at branding time. You never could get the stink of burning feathers out of your clothes.

Crossing the Beaverhead River was quite a trick. Once you get cattle in the river they'll just head for the other side. But *ducks* . . . they'd just as soon float downstream. Took us a whole day to cross the Beaverhead and round up the strays.

One night we camped outside Dillon under a full moon. The flock was pretty restless anyway, but then this yahoo from town came driving out in a Sears Roadster. When he shut that thing down, it cut loose with a backfire that sent the whole flock into a full stampede. Before we could get on our ponies and head 'em off, they'd stampeded down Main Street, waddled through every garden in town, and were terrorizing the inhabitants of the State Normal College. It took us all night to round

them suckers up. There wasn't a garden in Dillon that survived. The streets were a mess. There were even feathers on the arc lights.

I had an old pony named Shorty. I guess most duckboys named their ponies Shorty. Duck ponies are a breed apart. You don't see them around anymore. They were strong and husky, but short-legged, so you could get close to your work. Guys used to say that duck ponies were a cross between an Appaloosa and a basset hound. A feller's boots would take a real beating from rocks and prickly pear and sagebrush, because your feet rode so close to the ground.

When we'd loaded the whole flock into rail cars and sent them east, we got together with duck drovers from Twin Bridges and Whitehall, and even the gang from the Quack-Quack Cafe in Melrose, for a rodeo. Soapy Swanson and I took second in team roping. I caught that sucker around both wings in four seconds flat. Then I won first place in drake wrestling. I've still got the bite marks to show for it!

I liked being a duckboy, but I wasn't too sorry when it ended. I'd meet a gal in town and say "Howdy," but she'd smell feathers and she'd cross the street just to avoid me. Ah, those days are gone forever. Just as well.

TRAINING A BIRD DOG

DEPROGRAMMING A VEGETARIAN IN CATTLE COUNTRY

PLAYING "KICK THE CAN" WITH DAD

DOUBLE DATE OUT WEST

TESTING "ROADSIDE CAMOUFLAGE"

THE MORNING AFTER THE LAST DAY OF ELK SEASON

MONTANA REMOTE CONTROL

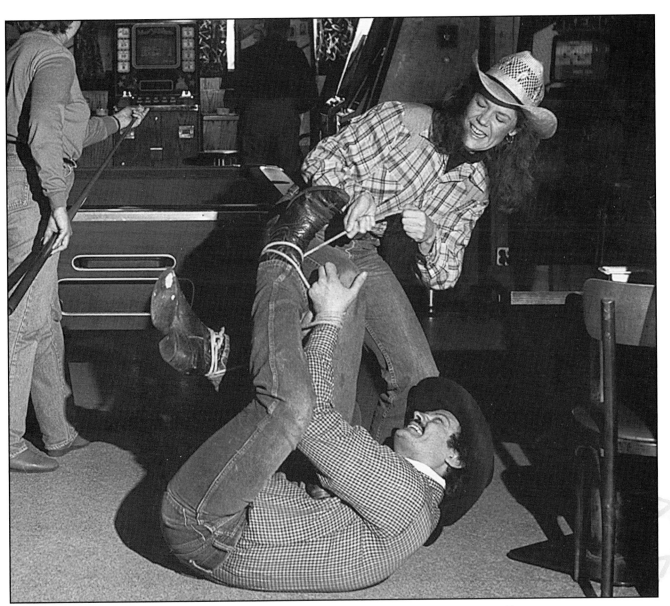

A GRADUATE OF THE COWGIRL ASSERTIVENESS-TRAINING PROGRAM

ZUCCHINI BEACH PARTY

SOUTH DAKOTA REST AREA

THIS SPUD'S FOR YOU!

A TRADITIONAL IDAHO GREETING

WESTERN GUN CONTROL

TROUTSKIING IN THE GREAT NORTHWEST

NORTHWEST 'COPTER LOGGER

Last Call for Bears

*T*his "Buy a Bear a Beer" Day business was fun at first, but things are getting out of hand. It started with a promotion by several bars along the Rocky Mountain Front, trying to boost business on slow days. They had all these bears wandering around outside of Augusta and Choteau, just getting into trouble. So bar owners figured, "Why not bring 'em in as new customers?" The trouble was, they couldn't pay . . . thus "Buy a Bear a Beer" Day.

A few beers didn't hurt anything, and the bruins would generally behave themselves. When they'd had too much, they just curled up next to the keno machines to sleep it off. "Most of 'em don't drive," explained Teton County deputy Ray Flatiron. "They're less trouble than the regulars."

Other bars around the West began to pick up on the practice, and soon it was as common as happy hour. "Buy a Bear a Beer" Day was edging out Sumo Night and Maggot Racing in popularity.

Before long, the bears began to hang around other days of the week, begging beers, pretzels, pickled eggs, and beer sausages. One big cinnamon bear would sleep under the porch at the Branding Iron Bar in Nederland, Colorado, and push his way in with the first customer, panhandling coffee and burgers. Boulder yuppies who visited the place Friday evenings felt that an inebriated old bear snoring and drooling on the hood of the Lexus provided more "atmosphere" than they'd bargained for.

One night in Darby, Montana, things got a little ugly. Two women from the West Fork got into a dispute over seating with a couple of bears. The bears got a little roughed up in the scuffle. Law enforcement was called, but it wasn't clear whether the town police or the Department of Fish, Wildlife and Parks had jurisdiction. By the time the cops arrived, the West Forkers were finishing their drinks, and the bears had gone home.

Winter didn't bring the expected lull in

EVERY WEDNESDAY IS "BUY A BEAR A BEER" DAY AT THE MINT BAR

activity. You can't blame the bears. Why spend the winter in a cave when there's a nice, warm saloon? They still hibernate, but only in fits and starts, and usually in the mens room. Who's going to tell a grizzly that he can't sleep ANYWHERE HE WANTS TO? Lack of sleep doesn't help the animals' dispositions, either. You don't know the meaning of "grouchy as a bear" until you run out of beer nuts in February.

The situation is out of control. I admit that many bar patrons have grown to know and love the shaggy barflies, even dressing them in hats and t-shirts with slogans like, "HUG ME . . . I'M AN ENDANGERED SPECIES." But bears are wild animals, and belong out under the stars . . . not under neon lights. If the bears won't leave voluntarily, bartenders could drive them out by serving Utah beer. It's time tavern owners put an end to this "Buy a Bear a Beer" Day nonsense, and concentrate on their paying customers. After all, you can't beat the thrill of maggot racing.

SOME OF NEVADA'S FAMOUS CAN-CAN DANCERS

THE TROUBLE WITH A SHORT HORSE IN THE ROCKIES

PRAIRIE DOG WATCHING . . . A POPULAR TOURIST ACTIVITY OUT WEST

COWBOY'S DESIGNATED DRIVER

ONE OF MINNESOTA'S FAMOUS "VIKING HAIRDRESSERS"

ONE OF THE LAST SURVIVING UPHILL-BOBSLED TEAMS

ROW VS. WADE: THE GREAT WESTERN FISHING CONTROVERSY

"IF YOU WAS THAT BIG OL' BUCK, WHERE WOULD YOU HIDE?"

SMOKING A WHITEFISH

MONTANA CARPOOL

"CHAINING UP" FOR WINTER FLYING IN THE ROCKIES

MONTANA POODLE

WHERE JERKY COMES FROM

ALONG MONTANA'S "INFORMATION SUPERHIGHWAY"

COME OUT WEST FOR A GOOD, STIFF CUP OF COFFEE

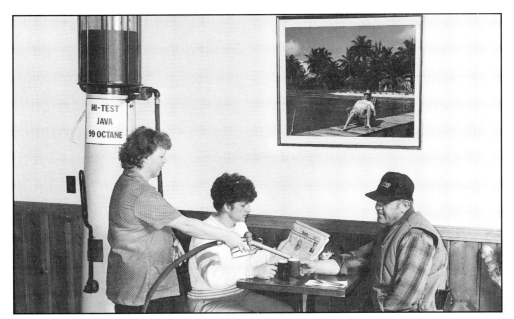

A Morning Fill-up at Don's Gas & Grub

Disposing of Leftover Cowboy Coffee: One of
the West's Most Hazardous Jobs

How To Make Cowboy Coffee

*—or camp coffee, or logger coffee...
it's all the same.*

*F*irst, dump cold water into the pot, over the old grounds. There's no need to rinse out the pot, unless you start to get more grounds than coffee. Throw the new coffee on top of the water, and put the fire to it. I use about a quarter cup of coffee to 2 cups water, unless I want it strong. Bob McDougall told me it should just float a spoon. A few moments of boiling are enough, unless you're Irish, Finnish, Salish, or Norwegian, in which case you'll probably let it sputter for 5 minutes or so.

To settle the grounds, dribble about a half-cup of cold water into the pot. For a big trail-crew-sized pot, settle the grounds by breaking a raw egg into it. Then fish the egg out and feed it to the dog. If the dog doesn't die, there's a chance the coffee's safe to drink. Some folks strain their coffee, but I prefer mine chunky style.

You have to drink logger coffee fast, to keep it from settin' up. It's no fun chipping it out of your cup with a jackknife.

Another thing—you can't make good camp coffee in a new coffeepot. You need an experienced, battered one with a colorful history. Mine's black on the inside and rusty on the outside, and covered with campfire soot. It's from a hunting cabin that my Dad and Doc Taylor owned up Tolan Creek in the '50s. When I was a kid, Dad and I hiked in, so he could show the cabin to me before some pinhead in the Forest Service canceled the lease and burned it. Years later, I located the cabin site and retrieved the coffeepot. Dad was glad to see it, because he hated to see a good coffeepot go to waste, even if it had been out in the weather for 20 years.

After I got married, my wife cleaned the coffeepot. Not only did it take six months to get the flavor back, I had to use a half pound of brazing rod to patch all the holes that appeared in the bottom. NEVER wash a good coffeepot.

Camp coffee is best with eggs and sourdough pancakes. Westerners are very proud and protective of their sourdough cultures. Some have been kept alive since the gold rush days.

Captain Lite claims he once had to destroy a wild sourdough culture. He says it was sneaking out at night. He got suspicious when the neighbors' dogs and cats began to disappear.

BATTLING A WILD SOURDOUGH CULTURE . . . ONE OF
THE HAZARDS OF RANCH COOKING

WYOMING'S ALL-STAR WATER HOCKEY TEAM

OREGON 3-PIECE SUIT

"LIVING FURS" ARE THE LATEST RAGE IN THE COLORADO ROCKIES

IT'S NOT EASY BEING A TREE-HUGGER IN CALIFORNIA

"YEAH, LOU . . . IT'S A DEN ALRIGHT! . . . LOU?"

CATCH AND RELEASE FISHING OUT WEST

GRIZZLY BEAR ARTIFICIAL-INSEMINATION TEAM

THE MILITIA GETS ITS FIRST BATTLESHIP

CATCH AND RELEASE BIG GAME HUNTING

LOW-TECH CHAIR LIFT

FISHING FOR STEELHEAD IN IDAHO

DISCOUNT AUTOMATIC DISHWASHER

ARIZONA FIRE HYDRANT?

MINNESOTA CARPOOL

BOULDER-SURFING: NOT FOR THE FAINT-HEARTED

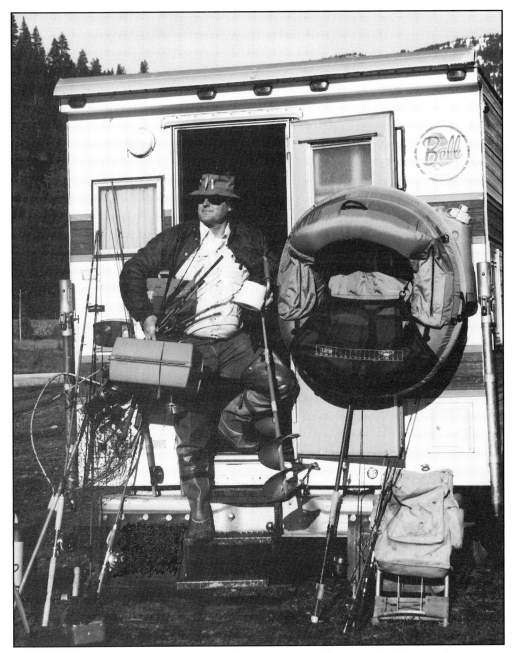

When the Goin' Gets Tough, the Tough Go Fishin'

A FEW OF THE BOYS "GETTING IN TOUCH WITH THEIR FEELINGS"

"Pumping Iron" Back at the Ranch

EATING GRANOLA BACK AT THE RANCH

DISCUSSING WATER RIGHTS—A WESTERN PASTIME

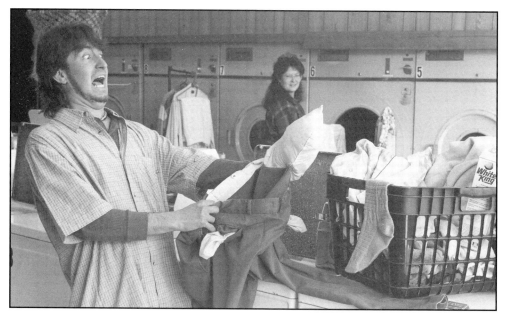

WHEN DOING YOUR LAUNDRY, ALWAYS CHECK FOR POCKET GOPHERS

IDAHO'S OLYMPIC FENCING TEAM

TROPHY GOPHER HUNTING IN NEVADA

ROCKY MOUNTAIN HEIST

NORTH DAKOTA TRASH COMPACTOR

COWBOY COMMUTERS

ROAD HUNTER

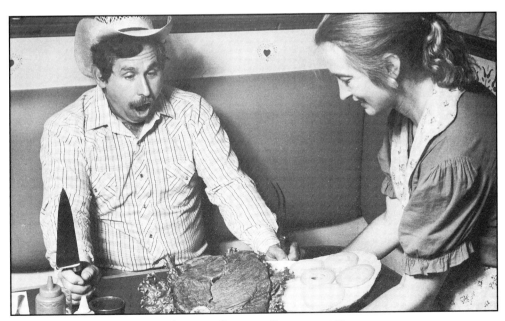

TEXAS STEAK SANDWICH

Do-It-Yourself Hearing Aids

DISCOUNT LAUNDROMAT

PLANTING POTATOES IN MINNESOTA

IT'S EASY TO SPOT THE "TURISTA" IN A NEW MEXICO CAFE

STRESS-MANAGEMENT SEMINAR

PASSIVE SOLAR COLLECTORS

GOOD HUNTING, BAD TIMING

FRESH MOOSE MILK: A "REAL MAN'S DRINK" IN WYOMING

So You Want To Be a Mountain Man?

*T*he West today has many more Mountain Men than roamed its forests and coulees in the 1840s. They're everywhere—on the streets, in the gas stations, in the bars, even (rarely) in the mountains. It's not, however, a life one can just jump into. You need the proper equipment, and there are rules to follow.

WHAT YOU NEED

1. An Income—Gone are the days when a Mountain Man could subsist on hunting and trapping. You need a steady income that allows you to pursue the Mountain Man lifestyle full time. Out-of-state unemployment claims are a favorite source, until they run out. You'll have to come into the office once a week to file your claim, and do a job search (asking for work as a brain surgeon or zeppelin mechanic) but the rest of the time is your own. A trust fund or pension is even better.

2. Buckskins—These are available for about $2,000 at any good Mountain Man supply outlet.

3. Guns—(the more, the better) It's nice if some of them will shoot, but most important is that they look impressive when carried in public, and they must complement the buckskins.

4. Knives—(large and conspicuous) These should be carried at all times, especially in public. You never know when you might have to skin a griz' in the men's room. They're also handy for personal grooming, flipping beer nuts into the mouth, slicing pickled eggs, and removing ticks. A tomahawk is also a handsome accessory, but is not required.

5. A Rig—This is nearly always a rough-looking 4-wheel-drive pickup. If it's a late model, don't worry. Just keep it really muddy and maybe nobody will notice.

6. Rig Hounds—No self-respecting Mountain Man would be without at least two large, mean dogs, with names like "Griz," "Lobo," or "Bear." If possible, get dogs that are mean only to *other people.* Their breed is unimportant, as long as they're part wolf, or can pass for such. These dogs spend most of their time in the back of the rig, snarling at, and hopefully intimidating, passers-by.

7. A "Camp"—Whether a cabin, RV, teepee, bus, or mobile home, it must be remote and properly landscaped. If your driveway is too passable, drive your rig back and forth on it in the rain until you remedy the problem. Landscaping usually includes mechanical refuse, animal parts, and signs warning of horrible penalties for trespassers.

DO'S AND DON'T'S

DO cultivate a practiced sneer, and learn the Mountain Man Persona. Get a video of *Jeremiah Johnson* and learn it by heart. Keep in mind, however, that Robert Redford is an environmentalist Hollywood Pretty Boy who probably eats with a fork. Grow lots of hair, clean your fingernails with your belt knife, and growl at others. Pull your hat down and scowl a lot. Then you'll be on track.

DON'T associate with non-Mountain Men. Locals are especially off-limits. They won't take you seriously, and may even laugh and point. Also, stay away from the "Rendezvous" crowd. They're part-timers—history buffs with real jobs, families, and lives. Most eat with a fork.

DO tell everyone who'll listen that you were "born 100 years too late." If another Mountain Man says he was born 100 years too late, reply "Oh yeah? Well, I was born *200* years too late!"

DON'T spend too much time in the mountains. There's nobody there to impress, it's often cold and wet up there, and it cuts into your bar time.

DO let it be known that you "kill and eat everything that walks, crawls, flies, or swims." Roadkill is OK, too.

DON'T kill anything legally or in season. It sets a bad precedent.

DO return quietly to the city to build a "grub-stake" when your money runs out.

. . . and above all . . . **DON'T** let anyone Out West see you working a regular job. It spoils the whole effect.

Drawing by Mike Gouse

IDAHO'S FAMOUS "SPUDYEAR BLIMP"

ARLENE'S EXERCISE BIKE

LARRY AND EARL'S NEW FISHFINDER

IN NASTY WEATHER, REMEMBER TO WEAR YOUR MACKINAW

WAITING FOR BREAKFAST

WINTER FLY-FISHING

TROLLING FOR GEESE IN SOUTH DAKOTA

FLOYD TRIES ICE FISHING

TEACHING "BEEFAEROBICS," THE LATEST ATTEMPT
TO RAISE LEANER BEEF

UTAH FOOD PROCESSOR

CHOCOLATE SPUDSICLES: A SUMMERTIME TREAT IN IDAHO

SQUASH TOURNAMENT

WATERFALL-SKIING: NO SPORT FOR SISSIES

ONE OF THE WEST'S TOUGHER GOLF HOLES

"LIFE IN THE FROST LANE" IN MINNESOTA

A FAMILY OF FOUR IN COLORADO

NORTH DAKOTA HONEYMOON SUITE

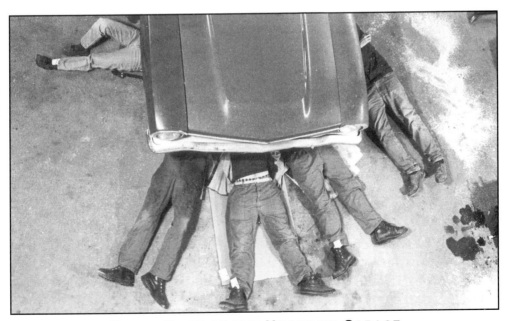

POKER NIGHT AT THE MILLTOWN GARAGE

NEW MEXICO FISHING GEAR

GOING TO THE DOGS

COWBOY HOT TUB

TRAINING FOR POLITICS

COWGIRL PEDICURE

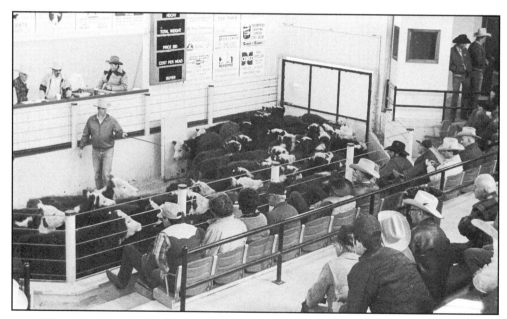

ON THE TRADING FLOOR OF THE MONTANA STOCK EXCHANGE

MONTANA MINI-STORAGE

COLORADO COMMUTER

PLAYING "ROUNDUP" WITH UNCLE BOB

TEX'S LONGHORN COW PONY

NEW MEXICO FAST FOOD

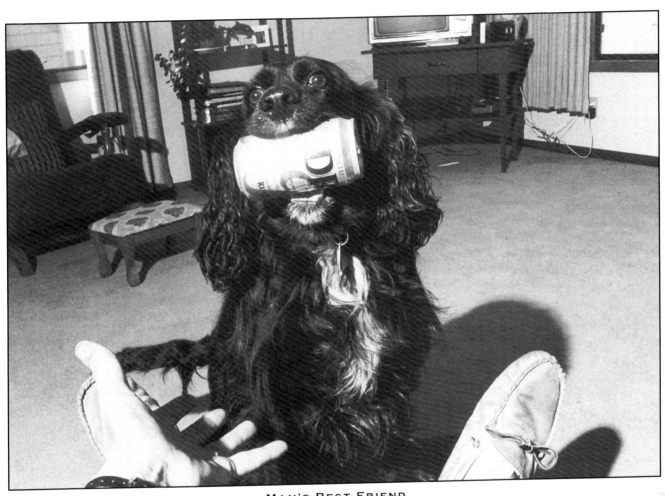

MAN'S BEST FRIEND

TEXAS BASS PLUG

SURVIVING HUNTING SEASON

THANKSGIVING IN THE GREAT NORTHWEST

BIG MUD WAGON, A WESTERNER'S B.M.W.

"MORE CALIFORNIANS, NO DOUBT"

AT THE RAISED-BY-WOLVES FAMILY REUNION

OVERDOSED ON FUN